CONTENTS

2B

LET'S GO
to the English World

UNIT 1 Are You Scared?

Mini Talk Look and listen. ▶

Are you scared?

Yes, I am.

No, I'm not.

Haha!

Dad, I'm scared.

WHOOSH!

Practice

A Listen and write the letter. 🎧 05   **B** Listen and repeat. 🎧 06

Are you happy?
Yes, I am.
No, I'm not. I'm angry.

1 happy ☐

2 sad ☐

3 hungry ☐

4 thirsty ☐

5 angry ☐

6 sleepy ☐

7 tired ☐

8 scared ☐

Listen & Talk

Listen and number. 🎧07

4

Write & Talk

A Listen, write, and read. 08

not	tired	Are
am	hungry	

Are you _____?

Yes, I _____.

I'm _____, too.

I'm sorry, Amy.

That's okay.

_____ you angry?

No, I'm _____ angry.

B Look and write. Then say.

scared	thirsty	sleepy	happy

1 I'm not sad. I'm _____.

2 I'm not tired. I'm _____.

3 I'm not angry. I'm _____.

4 I'm not hungry. I'm _____.

Story

A Listen, write, and read. ▶ 🎧 09

1. Are you _____, Sam?
   Yes, I am.

2. I'm sorry, Mom. _____ angry?
   No, I'm not _____.

3. Sorry. Are you sad?
   _____

4. Are you scared?
   _____

5. I'm _____!

6. Are you okay?
   Yes, I am.

scared   happy   angry   No, I'm not.   Yes, I am.   Are you

B Read and check.

1 Are you happy?

☐ Yes, I am.
☐ No, I'm not.

2 Are you angry?

☐ Yes, I am.
☐ No, I'm not.

3

☐ I'm scared.   ☐ I'm not scared.

Challenge

Draw and write.

Are _____ _____?

Yes, _____ _____.

Check-Up

A Listen and circle ○ or ×. 🎧11

1

○   ×

2

○   ×

3

○   ×

B Listen and match. 🎧12

1   **2**   **3**   **4**

C Listen and choose. 🎧13

1

ⓐ Yes, I am.

ⓑ No, I'm not.

2

ⓐ Yes, I am.

ⓑ No, I'm not.

3

ⓐ Yes, I am.

ⓑ No, I'm not.

D Look, check, and write.

1

I'm not okay. _____

☐ I'm angry. ☐ I'm tired.

2

A: Are you _____?

☐ scared ☐ sleepy

B: Yes, I am.

3

A: Are you hungry?

B: _____

☐ Yes, I am. ☐ No, I'm not.

E Write and say.

1

Yes, I am.

2

Are you thirsty?

Mini Talk Look and listen.

What are these?

They're baby lions.

What are those?

They're monkeys.

CHECK 17 1 a ☐ b ☐ 2 a ☐ b ☐

10

Practice

A Listen and write the letter. 18   **B** Listen and repeat. 19

What are these? | They're monkeys.

1 monkeys ☐

giraffes ☐ 4

2

pandas ☐

3

kangaroos ☐

What are those? | They're lions.

8

5

6

snakes ☐ 7

lions ☐

zebras ☐

elephants ☐

Listen & Talk

(A) Listen and circle. 🎧 20

Write & Talk

A Listen, write, and read. 🎧 21

duck	pandas	monkey
kangaroos	those	this

What are _____?

They're _____.

What's that?

It's a _____.

What's _____?

It's a _____.

What are these?

They're _____.

B Circle and write. Then ask and answer.

What are those?

What's that?

1 (They're / It's) _____.

2 (They're / It's) _____.

3 (They're / It's) _____.

4 (They're / It's) _____.

a rabbit   a giraffe   elephants   zebras

Story

A Listen, write, and read. ▶ 🎧22

1

What's that?

It's a _____.

2

What are _____?

They're _____.

3

What's this?

It's an _____.

4

What are _____?

They're _____.

5

They're my friends.

Hello!

6

Oops!

---

these   those   elephant   snake   monkeys   zebras

B Read and match.

1

What's this?

They're monkeys.

2

What are those?

They're zebras.

3

What are these?

It's an elephant.

Guess and write.

What's this?

_____

What are these?

_____

A Listen and choose. 24

1

ⓐ   ⓑ

2

ⓐ   ⓑ

3

ⓐ   ⓑ

B Listen and match. 25

1
2
3
4

C Listen and number. 26

D Look, circle, and write.

1

_____ elephants. (It's / They're)

_____ a duck. (It's / They're)

2

A: What are _____? (these / those)

B: They're _____. (lions / pandas)

3

A: What are _____? (these / those)

B: They're _____. (kangaroos / giraffes)

E Write and say.

1

What are these?

2

They're zebras.

Review 1

A) Look and write.

giraffe	thirsty	snake	scared	monkey
sleepy	happy	kangaroo	panda	

1

_____

2

_____

3

_____

4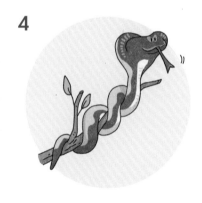

_____

5

_____

6

_____

7

_____

8

_____

9

_____

B Circle and check.

hungry | happy   tired | scared   sad | angry   thirsty | sleepy

1 Are you hungry? ☐ Yes, I am. ☐ No, I'm not.

2 Are you scared? ☐ Yes, I am. ☐ No, I'm not.

3 Are you sad? ☐ Yes, I am. ☐ No, I'm not.

4 Are you thirsty? ☐ Yes, I am. ☐ No, I'm not.

C Circle and write.

these | those   these | those   these | those   these | those

1 A: What are _____? 2 A: What are _____?

   B: They're _____.   B: They're _____.

3 A: What are _____? 4 A: What are _____?

   B: They're _____.   B: They're _____.

giraffes
zebras
lions
elephants

Is It a Kite?

Mini Talk Look and listen.

Practice

A Listen and write the letter. 🎧31   **B** Listen and repeat. 🎧32

| Is it a bat? | Yes, it is. |
| | No, it isn't. It's a bike. |

1 **2** **3** **4**

baseball ☐   soccer ball ☐   bat ☐   glove ☐

scooter ☐   bike ☐   kite ☐   jump rope ☐

5 **6** **7** **8**

Listen & Talk

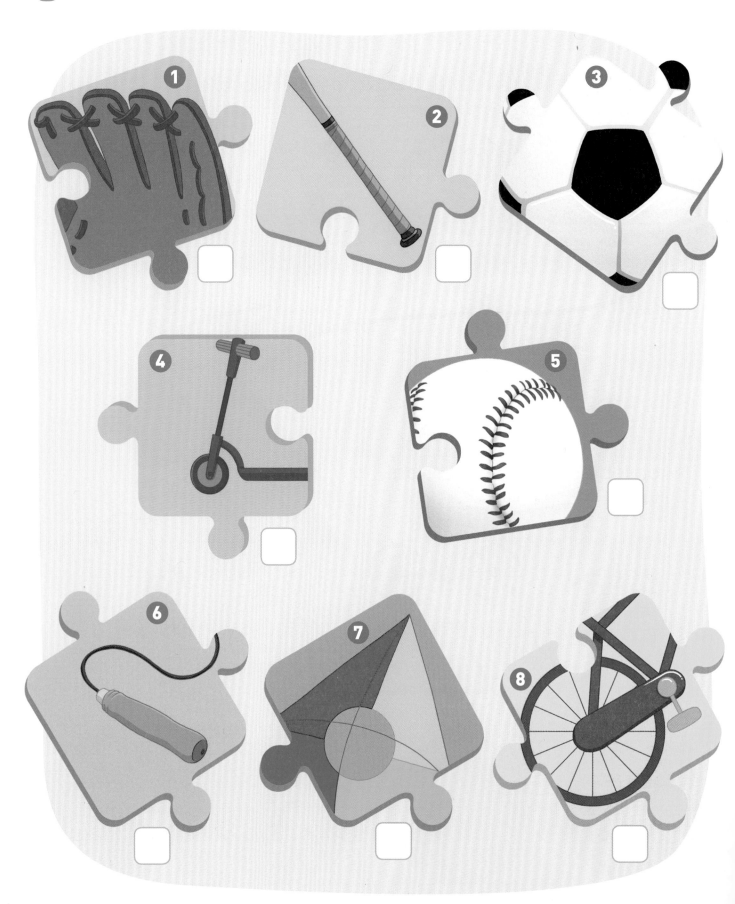

Write & Talk

A Listen, write, and read. 🎧 34

snake	scooter
it	Yes	isn't

🧒 This is for you, Elsa.

👧 Is it a _____?

🧒 _____, it is.

👧 Thank you, Mom.

🧒 Is _____ an elephant?

👧 No, it _____.

🧒 What is it?

👧 It's a _____.

B Stick and write. Then ask and answer.

Yes, it is.

No, it isn't.

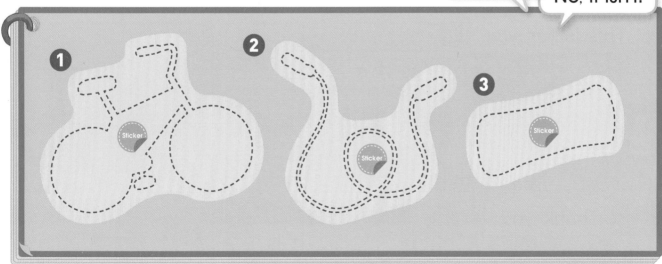

1 Is it a bike?

_____, _____.

2 Is it a baseball?

_____, _____.

3 Is it a pencil case?

_____, _____.

Story

A Listen, write, and read. ▶ 🎧 35

1. Here it is.
   Thank you!

2. What is it?
   Is it a _____?
   No, it isn't.

3. Is it a _____?
   No, it _____.

4. Is it a _____?
   No, it isn't.

5. This is for you.
   Thank you.

6. Is it a _____?
   _____, it is.

7. I like it.

| bike | soccer ball | jump rope | scooter | Yes | isn't |

24

B **Read and match.**

1  •

• Is it a scooter? •

• Yes, it is.

2  •

• Is it a jump rope? •

• No, it isn't.

3 •

• Is it a bike? •

Challenge

Look and write. Then color.

Is it a glove?

Is it a bike?

_____, _____.

_____, _____.

It's a _____.

36 Song

Check-Up

A Listen and mark ○ or ✕. 🎧37

1

2

3

B Listen and choose. 🎧38

1
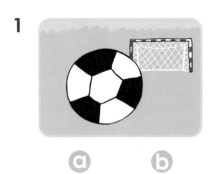
ⓐ   ⓑ

2

ⓐ   ⓑ

3
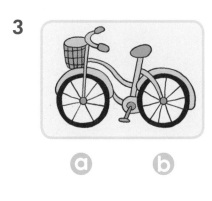
ⓐ   ⓑ

C Listen and match. 🎧39

1
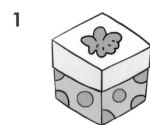

2

3
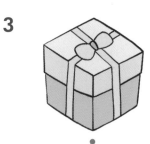

4
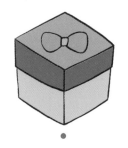

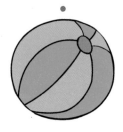

D Look, circle, and write.

1

A: Is it a _____?
       (bike / bat)

B: Yes, it is.

2

A: What is it? Is it a _____?
          (kite / glove)

B: Yes, it is.

3

A: Is it a baseball?

B: No, it isn't. It's a _____.
      (scooter / jump rope)

E Write and say.

1

Is it a bat?

2

Yes, it is.

UNIT 4 Are They Birds?

Mini Talk Look and listen. ▶ 🎧 42

Look! Are they birds?

Yes, they are.

Is it a frog?

Yes, it is.

CROAK!

CROAK!

🎧 43 CHECK 1 a b 2 a b

28

Practice

A Listen and write the letter. 🎧 44   **B** Listen and repeat. 🎧 45

Are they bees?
| Yes, they are. |
| No, they aren't. They're ladybugs. |

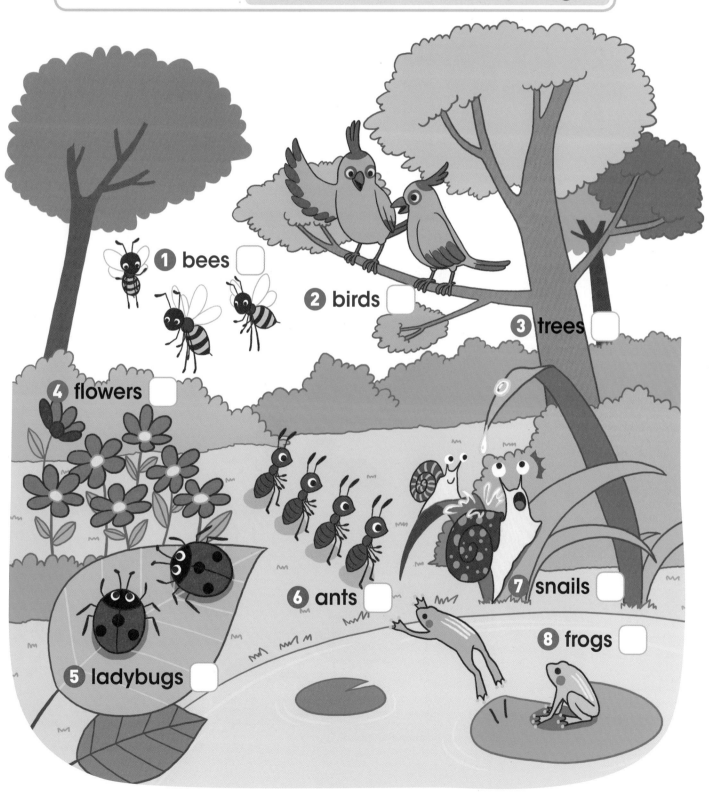

1 bees ☐

2 birds ☐

3 trees ☐

4 flowers ☐

5 ladybugs ☐

6 ants ☐

7 snails ☐

8 frogs ☐

Listen & Talk

A Listen and mark ○ or X. 🎧 46

Write & Talk

A Listen, write, and read. 🎧 47

Are _____ bees?

No, they aren't.

What are they?

They're _____.

Is it _____?

Yes, it is.

Are they _____?

Yes, they are.

B Look and write. Then ask and answer.

Yes, they are.

No, they aren't.

1   Are they trees?

_____, _____.

2   Are they giraffes?

_____, _____.

3   Are they zebras?

_____, _____.

4   Are they ladybugs?

_____, _____.

Story

A Listen, write, and read. ▶ 48

a snail   a rabbit   trees   ants   ladybugs

B Read and match.

1

Are they ants?

No, it isn't.
It's a rabbit.

2

Are they bees?

No, they aren't.
They're ladybugs.

3

Is it a snake?

Yes, they are.

Challenge

Look and write.

1

2

_____

Yes, they are.

Are they trees?

_____ They're _____.

Check-Up

A Listen and choose. 🎧 50

1

ⓐ ⓑ

2

ⓐ ⓑ

3

ⓐ ⓑ

B Listen and match. 🎧 51

1 🔊
2 🔊
3 🔊
4 🔊

C Listen and choose. 🎧 52

1

2

3

34

D Circle and write.

1

A: Are they _____?
       (flowers / trees)

B: Yes, they are.

2

A: Are they bees?

B: No, they aren't. They're _____.
       (ladybugs / birds)

3

A: _____
  (Are they snails? / Is it a snail?)

B: Yes, it is.

E Write and say.

1

A: Are they frogs?

B: _____

2

A: _____

B: Yes, they are.

Review 2

Ⓐ Write and number.

b i __ e	5
g __ o __ e	
__ i __ e	
s __ o o __ e r	
b a __ e __ a l l	

	__ n __
	b __ __ __
	l __ d y b __ g
	f r __ __ __
	s n __ __ l

36

Ⓑ **Look and write.**

| Yes, it is. | No, it isn't. | Yes, they are. | No, they aren't. |

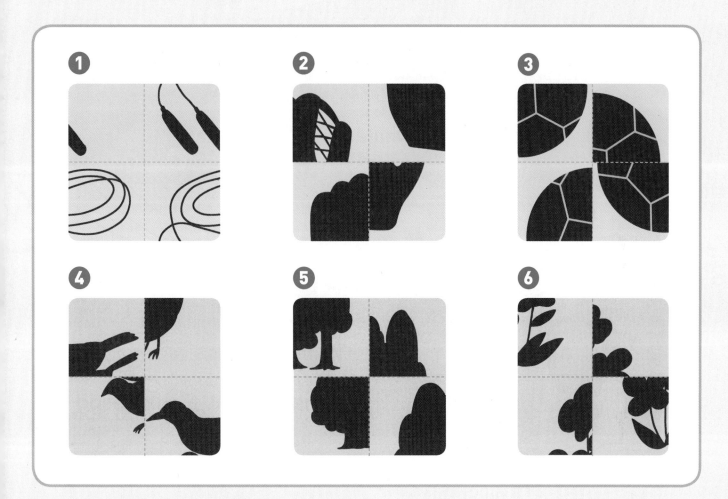

1 A: Is it a jump rope?

B: _____

2 A: Is it a bat?

B: _____

3 A: Is it a baseball?

B: _____

4 A: Are they frogs?

B: _____

5 A: Are they giraffes?

B: _____

6 A: Are they flowers?

B: _____

Look at the Whale

Mini Talk Look and listen. ▶ 55

Look at the whale.

Wow! It's big.

Look at the turtle. It's small.

It's cute.

56 CHECK 1 a ☐ b ☐ 2 a ☐ b ☐

Practice

A Listen and write the letter. 🎧57   **B** Listen and repeat. 🎧58

| Look at the whale. | It's big. | It's small. |

1 whale ☐

2 shrimp ☐

3 starfish ☐

4 shark ☐

5 jellyfish ☐

6 crab ☐

7 turtle ☐

8 seahorse ☐

Listen & Talk

A Listen, number, and match. 🎧 59

big   small

Write & Talk

small   big
crabs   bird

A Listen, write, and read. 🎧 60

👦 Look at the _____.

Wow! It's _____.

👧 I'm scared.

👧 Look! Are they _____?

👦 Yes, they are.

👧 They're very _____.

👦 Yes, they're cute, too.

B Write and circle. Then say.

1 Look at the _____.
It's (big / small).

2 Look at the _____.
They're (big / small).

3 Look at the _____.
It's (big / small).

turtles   elephant   starfish

Story

Ⓐ Listen, write, and read. ▶ 🎧61

1. Look at the _____. — It's big.

2. Look at the fish. — They're _____.

3. Look at the _____. — Wow, it's very _____.

4. Look at the _____. — It's small and cute.

5. It's big. Is it a _____?

6. Yes, it is.

7. It's fun.

| turtle | shark | seahorse | jellyfish | big | small |

B Read and match.

1 Look at the fish. •

• They're small.

2 Look at the shark. •

• It's big.

3 Look at the turtle. •

• It's very big.

Challenge

Stick and write.

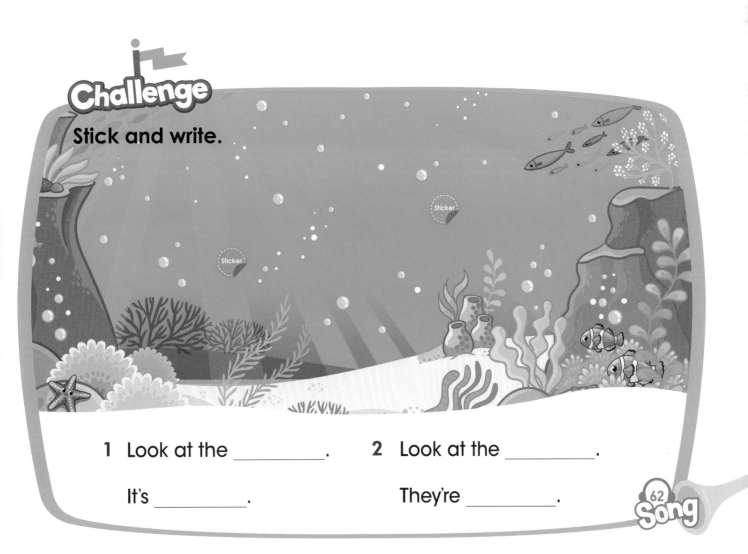

1 Look at the _____.

   It's _____.

2 Look at the _____.

   They're _____.

62 Song

Check-Up

A Listen and number. 🎧 63

B Listen and choose. 🎧 64

1 ⓐ
   ⓑ

2 ⓐ
   ⓑ

3 ⓐ
   ⓑ

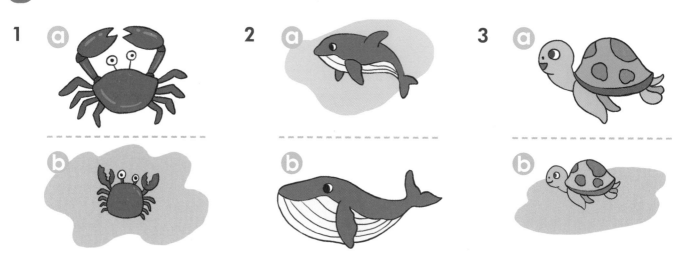

C Listen and circle ◯ or ✕. 🎧 65

1   2   3

◯ ✕   ◯ ✕   ◯ ✕

D Look, circle, and write.

1

A: Look at the _____.
(whale / jellyfish)

B: It's (big / small).

2

A: Look at the _____.
(crabs / turtles)

B: They're (big / small).

3

A: Look at the _____.
(starfish / shrimp)

B: It's very (big / small).

E Write and say.

1

It's big.

2

Look at the crab.

Do You Have Red Paint?

Mini Talk Look and listen. ▶

Practice

A Listen and write the letter. 🎧 70   **B** Listen and repeat. 🎧 71

> I have paint.   I don't have paint.

1 paint ☐   **2** crayons ☐   **3** a marker ☐   **4** a paintbrush ☐

> Do you have tape?   Yes, I do.   No, I don't.

5 ☺ tape ☐   **6** ☹ paper ☐   **7** ☺ a glue stick ☐   **8** ☹ scissors ☐

Listen & Talk

A Listen and draw ○ or ✗. 72

1

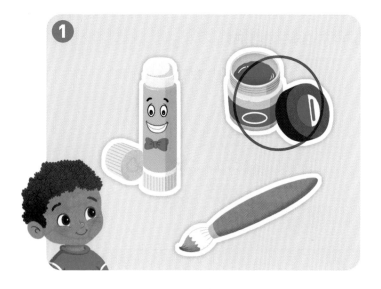

2

3

4

5

6

Write & Talk

A Listen, write, and read. 🎧 73

> do　have　don't
> crayons　a ruler

Do you have _____ ?

No, I don't.

But I _____ paint.

I _____ have a ruler.

Do you have _____ ?

Yes, I _____ . Here you are.

Thank you.

B Look and write. Then ask and answer.

Yes, I do.

No, I don't.

1 Do you have scissors?

_____ , _____ _____ .

2 Do you have a paintbrush?

_____ , _____ _____ .

3 Do you have a pencil?

_____ , _____ _____ .

Story

Ⓐ Listen, write, and read. ▶ 🎧74

1 Do you have blue _____?

Yes, I do.

2 Do you have a black crayon?

_____

3 Do you have _____?

Yes, I do.

4 I _____ tape. Do you have tape?

No, I don't.

5 I have _____.

A glue stick? Thanks.

6 Surprise!

7 Oops!

---

don't have   scissors   a glue stick   paint   Yes, I do.

B Read and circle.

1  I (have / don't have) blue paint.

2  I (have / don't have) scissors.

3  I (have / don't have) tape.

Challenge

Stick and write.

I have ...

I don't have ...

I have _____.

But I don't have _____.

Check-Up

A Listen and choose. 🎧76

1
ⓐ
ⓑ

2
ⓐ
ⓑ

3
ⓐ
ⓑ

B Listen, match, and circle. 🎧77

1

2

3

4

Yes   No

Yes   No

Yes   No

Yes   No

C Listen and number. 🎧78

D Read and write.

1

I have paper.

But I _____ scissors.

2

A: Do you have _____?

B: Yes, I do. Here you are.

3

A: Do you have a red marker?

B: _____

E Write and say.

1
Do you have a glue stick?

2

Yes, I do.

Review 3

A Match and write.

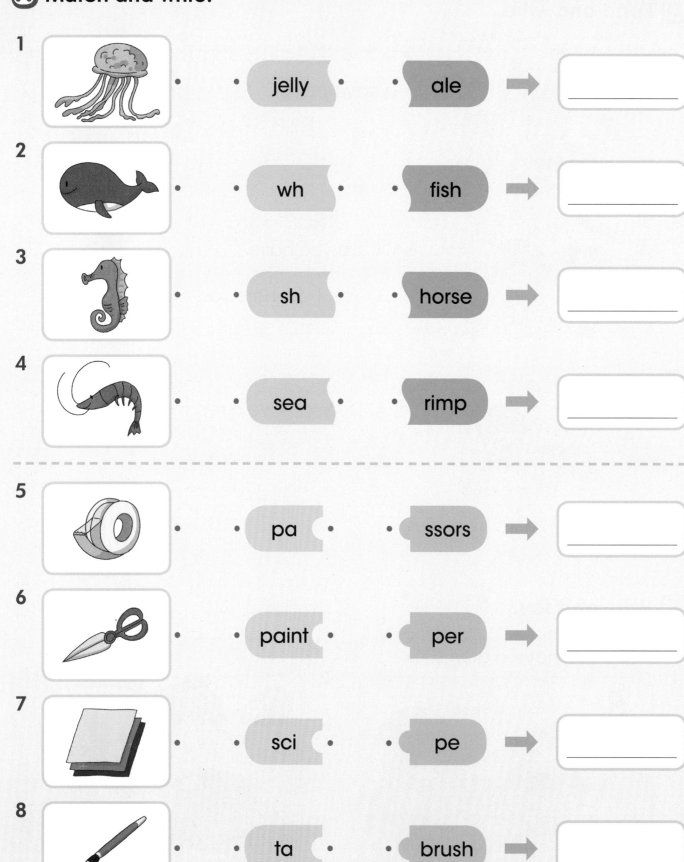

1. jelly · · ale → _____

2. wh · · fish → _____

3. sh · · horse → _____

4. sea · · rimp → _____

5. pa · · ssors → _____

6. paint · · per → _____

7. sci · · pe → _____

8. ta · · brush → _____

B **Write and check.**

shark

crab

turtle

starfish

1 A: Look at the _____.

 B: ☐ It's big. ☐ It's small.

2 A: Look at the _____.

 B: ☐ It's big. ☐ It's small.

3 A: Look at the _____.

 B: ☐ It's big. ☐ It's small.

4 A: Look at the _____.

 B: ☐ It's big. ☐ It's small.

glue stick

paint

marker

crayons

5 A: Do you have _____?

 B: ☐ Yes, I do. ☐ No, I don't.

6 A: Do you have _____?

 B: ☐ Yes, I do. ☐ No, I don't.

7 A: Do you have a _____?

 B: ☐ Yes, I do. ☐ No, I don't.

8 A: Do you have a _____?

 B: ☐ Yes, I do. ☐ No, I don't.

What Do You Like?

Mini Talk Look and listen. ▶ 🎧81

Practice

A Listen and write the letter. 🎧83   **B** Listen and repeat. 🎧84

What do you like?   I like grapes.

1 grapes ☐
2 oranges ☐
3 peaches ☐
4 carrots ☐
5 potatoes ☐
6 onions ☐
7 tomatoes ☐
8 mushrooms ☐

Listen & Talk

Ⓐ Listen and match. 🎧 85

1

2

3

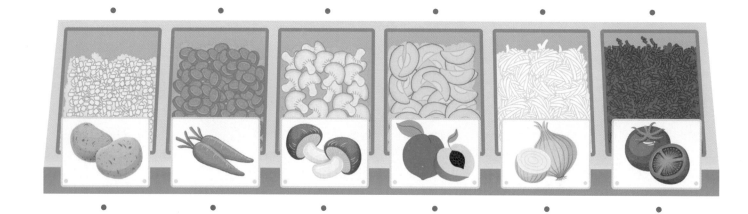

4

5

6

Write & Talk

A Listen, write, and read. 🎧 86

like   What   carrots
peaches   potatoes

Do you like _____?

No, I don't _____ peaches.

I like apples.

Do you like _____?

No, I don't.

_____ do you like?

I like _____.

B Look and write. Then ask and answer.

I like ...

I don't like ...

1 Do you like tomatoes?

_____, _____ _____.

2 Do you like mushrooms?

_____, _____ _____.

3 Do you like pears?

_____, _____ _____.

Story

A Listen, write, and read.

1. What do you like? / I like _____.
2. _____ do you like? / I like _____.
3. Do you like _____? / Yes, I do.
4. I don't like tomatoes. I don't like mushrooms. I don't like potatoes.
5. Onions!
6. Do you like _____? / Yes, I do.
7. Excuse me.

onions   tomatoes   potatoes   mushrooms   What

B Read and match.

What do you like?

1  • • I like tomatoes. •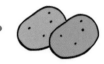

2  • • I like potatoes. •

3  • • I like onions. •

Challenge

Choose two things and write.

I _____ _____.

But I _____ _____.

88 Song

Check-Up

A Listen and choose. 🎧89

1

ⓐ   ⓑ

2

ⓐ   ⓑ

3
ⓐ   ⓑ

B Listen and draw. 🎧90

1   **2**   **3**   **4**

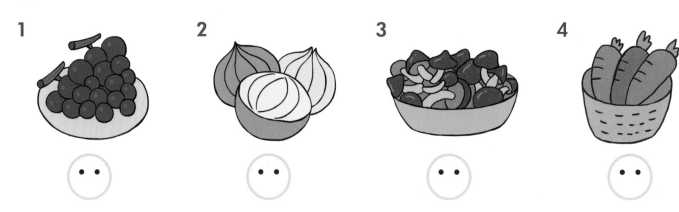

C Listen and choose. 🎧91

1

2

3

D Look and write.

1

I _____ peaches.

But I _____ grapes.

2

A: I like mushrooms. _____ do you like?

B: I like _____.

3

A: Do you like onions?

B: _____

E Write and say.

1

Yes, I do.

2

What do you like?

UNIT 8 Can You Swim?

Mini Talk Look and listen. ▶ 🎧94

Practice

A Listen and write the letter. 🎧 96

B Listen and repeat. 🎧 97

Can you **dive**? | Yes, I can. | No, I can't.

1 dive ▢

2 swim ▢

3 ski ▢

4 skate ▢

5 run fast ▢

6 jump rope ▢

7 sing well ▢

8 dance well ▢

Listen & Talk

(A) Listen, match, and draw. 🎧 98

Write & Talk

A Listen, write, and read. 🎧 99

Can you _____?

No, I _____.

_____ you run fast, Roy?

Yes, I can.

I can't dance well.

But I can _____. Listen!

Good! I can _____.

B Look and write. Then say.

swim   skate   ski   dive

I can't _____.

But I can _____.

I _____.

But I _____ _____.

Story

Ⓐ Listen, write, and read. ▶ 🎧100

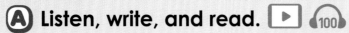

1 Can you _____?

Yes, I can.

2 I can _____, too.

Look!

Great!

3 I can skate.
Can you _____?

No, I can't.

4 I _____ swim.

Aha!

I can't skate.

5 I can't _____.
Can you jump?

Yes, I _____ jump.

6 Wow, great!

| can | can't | skate | dive | jump | swim |

68

B Read and circle.

1

Can you dive?

Yes, I can dive. / No, I can't dive.

2

Can you skate?

Yes, I can skate. / No, I can't skate.

3

Can you jump?

Yes, I can jump. / No, I can't jump.

What can you do? Circle and write.

can
can't

can
can't

can
can't

can
can't

can
can't

1 Can you ski?

2 Can you jump rope?

_____, _____ _____.

_____, _____ _____.

Check-Up

A Listen and choose. 🎧102

1
ⓐ ⓑ

2
ⓐ ⓑ

3
ⓐ ⓑ

B Listen, number, and circle. 🎧103

Yes No

Yes No

Yes No

Yes No

C Listen and match. 🎧104

1

2

3

•   •

•   •

•   •

•   •

•   •

•   •

can can't

can can't

can can't

D Look and write.

1

I _____ swim.

But I _____ run fast.

2

A: Can you jump rope?

B: _____

3

A: Can you sing well?

B: _____

E Write and say.

1

Can you ski?

2

No, I can't.

A Circle and write.

1

peaches

grapes

_____

2

tomatoes

oranges

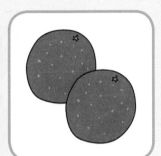

_____

3

onions

carrots

_____

4

mushrooms

potatoes

_____

5

swim

dive

_____

6

skate

ski

_____

7

run fast

jump rope

_____

8

sing well

dance well

_____

B Look and write.

Yes, I do.

No, I don't.

I like grapes.

1 A: What do you like?

B: _____

2 A: Do you like potatoes?

B: _____

3 A: Do you like carrots?

B: _____

4 A: Do you like tomatoes?

B: _____

C Look and write.

1 A: Can you ski?

B: _____

2 A: Can you swim?

B: _____

Yes, I can.

No, I can't.

3 A: Can you dance well?

B: _____

4 A: Can you run fast?

B: _____

Songs

Unit 1 Are You Happy? 🎧10

Are you happy?

 Yes, I am. I'm happy.

Are you tired?

 No, I'm not. I'm hungry.

Are you sleepy?

 Yes, I am. I'm sleepy.

Unit 2 What Are These? 🎧23

What are these?

 They're pandas.

What are those?

 They're lions.

What are these?

 They're monkeys.

What are those?

 They're elephants.

Unit 3 Is It a Baseball? 🎧36

Is it a baseball?

 No, it isn't.

Is it a soccer ball?

 Yes! Yes, it is.

Is it a bike?

 No, it isn't.

Is it a scooter?

 Yes! Yes, it is. I like it.

Unit 4 Are They Ants? 🎧49

Are they ants?

 No, they aren't. They're bees.

Are they ladybugs?

 Yes, they are. I like ladybugs!

Are they snails?

 No, they aren't. They're frogs.

Unit 5 Look at the Whale

Look at the whale.

It's big.

Look at the starfish.

It's small.

Look at the shark.

It's big.

Look at the crab.

It's small. It's cute!

Unit 6 Do You Have Scissors? 75

I don't have a glue stick.

Do you have a glue stick?

Yes, I do. Here you are.

Thank you.

I don't have scissors.

Do you have scissors?

Yes, I do. Here you are.

Thank you.

Unit 7 What Do You Like? 88

I like grapes. What do you like?

I like peaches.

I like pineapples.

I like carrots. What do you like?

I like mushrooms.

I like onions.

Do you like onions?

Yes, I do.

Unit 8 Can You Swim?  101

I can swim. Can you swim?

Yes! Yes, I can.

Can you dive? Can you dive?

No! No, I can't.

I can ski. Can you ski?

Yes! Yes, I can.

Can you skate? Can you skate?

No! No, I can't.

Ⓐ Listen and repeat. Then read. 🎧105

a-e

1 c - ake ➜ cake

2 l - ake ➜ lake

3 g - ame ➜ game

4 t - ape ➜ tape

5 v - ase ➜ vase

6 l - ate ➜ late

Ⓑ Listen and circle. 🎧106

1
late
cake
tape

2
game
lake
vase

3
vase
tape
cake

4
late
name
lake

Ⓒ Match and write.

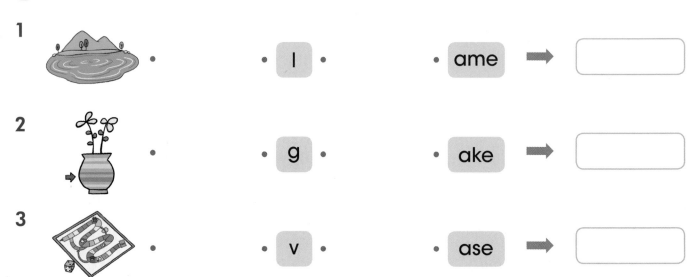

1 • • l • • ame ➜ [____]

2 • • g • • ake ➜ [____]

3 • • v • • ase ➜ [____]

Ⓐ Listen and repeat. Then read. 🎧107

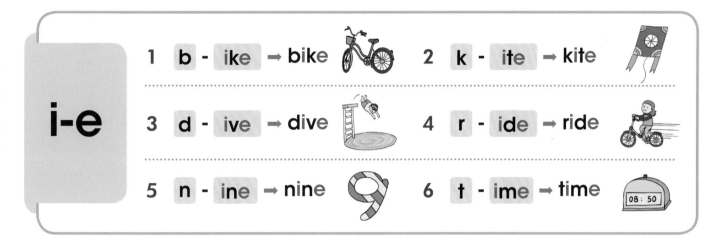

i-e

1 b - ike ➡ bike

2 k - ite ➡ kite

3 d - ive ➡ dive

4 r - ide ➡ ride

5 n - ine ➡ nine

6 t - ime ➡ time

Ⓑ Listen and match. 🎧108

1 k •   • ide
   r •   • ite

2 d •   • ine
   n •   • ive

3 b •   • ike
   r •   • ide

4 t •   • ike
   l •   • ime

Ⓒ Unscramble and write.

1

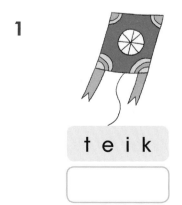

t e i k

2

i r e d

3

e d i v

Ⓐ Listen and repeat. Then read. 🎧109

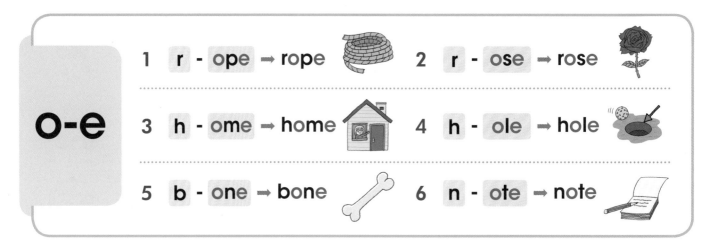

o-e

1 r - ope ➡ rope

2 r - ose ➡ rose

3 h - ome ➡ home

4 h - ole ➡ hole

5 b - one ➡ bone

6 n - ote ➡ note

Ⓑ Listen and circle. 🎧110

1 rope   note   rose

2 hole   bone   home

3 note   nose   hole

4 home   rope   bone

Ⓒ Circle and match.

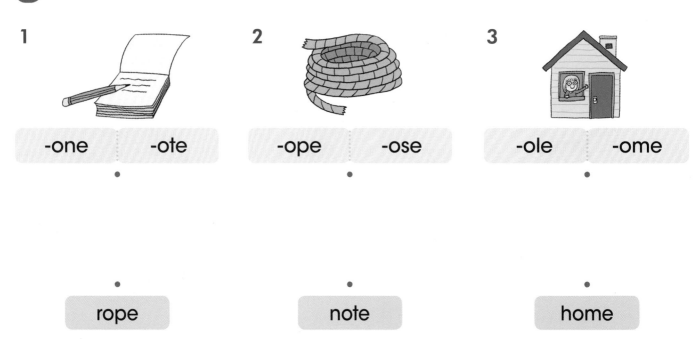

1   -one   -ote

2   -ope   -ose

3   -ole   -ome

rope

note

home

A Listen and repeat. Then read. 111

u-e

1 c - ube → cube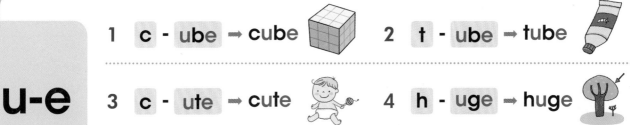

2 t - ube → tube

3 c - ute → cute

4 h - uge → huge

5 m - ule → mule

6 J - une → June

B Listen and circle. 112

1 huge
   cube
   June

2 cube
   cute
   tube

3 huge
   mule
   cube

4 June
   tube
   mule

C Match and write.

1  • • h • • ute ➡ [   ]

2  • • t • • uge ➡ [   ]

3  • • c • • ube ➡ [   ]

Ⓐ Listen, circle, and write. 🎧113

1
-ute   -ake
c_____

2
-ome   -ime
t_____

3
-ine   -ote
n_____

4
-ase   -ike
v_____

Ⓑ Listen, circle, and match. 🎧114

1
June
rose

2
cube
tape

3
tube
lake

4
nine
bone

Ⓒ Circle and write.

1

-ime   -ole

h_____

2

-ike   -ake

b_____

3

-ute   -ate

l_____

Phonics 6

A Listen and check. 🎧115

1
- ☐ fan
- ☐ map

2
- ☐ lake
- ☐ game

3
- ☐ big
- ☐ sit

4
- ☐ bike
- ☐ kite

5
- ☐ fox
- ☐ hot

6
- ☐ hole
- ☐ home

7
- ☐ cut
- ☐ run

8
- ☐ cute
- ☐ cube

B Listen, match, and write. 🎧116

1

t •   • ube

c •   • ub

_____

2

j •   • ame

g •   • am

_____

3

h •   • it

k •   • ite

_____

4

f •   • ope

r •   • ox

_____

C Read and circle.

1

pot   note

2

vase   bag

3

dive   mix

Ⓐ Listen and repeat. Then read. 🎧117

ch sh wh

1 ch → chin

2 ch → check

3 sh → ship

4 sh → shop

5 wh → whale

6 wh → white

Ⓑ Listen and check. 🎧118

1 ☐ ch ☐ sh ☐ wh

2 ☐ ch ☐ sh ☐ wh

3 ☐ ch ☐ sh ☐ wh

4 ☐ ch ☐ sh ☐ wh

Ⓒ Match and write.

1 • • sh • • ale → ☐

2 • • ch • • op → ☐

3 • • wh • • in → ☐

A Listen and repeat. Then read. 🎧119

th

1 th → this

2 th → that

3 th → those

4 th → thin

5 th → thick

6 th → three

B Listen and check. 🎧120

1
- ☐ thin
- ☐ that

2
- ☐ this
- ☐ three

3
- ☐ thick
- ☐ this

4
- ☐ three
- ☐ those

C Match and write.

1  th •
- • in
- • at

_____

2  th •
- • at
- • ick

_____

3  th •
- • is
- • in

_____

4  th •
- • ree
- • ose

_____

Word List 2B

Unit 1 Are You Scared?

angry   _____

happy   _____

hungry   _____

okay   _____

sad   _____

scared   _____

sleepy   _____

thirsty   _____

tired   _____

Unit 2 What Are These?

elephants   _____

giraffes   _____

kangaroos   _____

lions   _____

monkeys   _____

pandas   _____

snakes   _____

these   _____

they   _____

those   _____

zebras   _____

Unit 3 Is It a Kite?

baseball   _____

bat   _____

bike   _____

glove   _____

it   _____

jump rope   _____

kite   _____

pencil case   _____

scooter   _____

soccer ball   _____

Unit 4 Are They Birds?

ants   _____

bees   _____

birds   _____

flowers   _____

frogs   _____

giraffes   _____

ladybugs   _____

snails   _____

they   _____

trees   _____

zebras   _____

Unit 5 · Look at the Whale

big _____

crab _____

cute _____

fun _____

jellyfish _____

seahorse _____

shark _____

shrimp _____

small _____

starfish _____

turtle _____

very _____

whale _____

Unit 6 · Do You Have Red Paint?

a glue stick _____

a marker _____

a paintbrush _____

a pencil _____

a ruler _____

an eraser _____

have _____

crayons _____

paint _____

paper _____

scissors _____

tape _____

Unit 7 · What Do You Like?

apples _____

bananas _____

carrots _____

grapes _____

like _____

mushrooms _____

onions _____

oranges _____

peaches _____

pears _____

potatoes _____

tomatoes _____

Unit 8 · Can You Swim?

can _____

can't _____

dance well _____

dive _____

jump _____

jump rope _____

run fast _____

skate _____

ski _____

sing well _____

swim _____

Syllabus 2B

Unit 1　Are You Scared?

Structures	Vocabulary		Phonics
• Are you scared?　Yes, I am. / No, I'm not.	happy	sleepy	Long Vowel a-e
• I'm hungry.	sad	tired	
• I'm not hungry.	hungry	scared	
• I'm sorry. That's okay.	thirsty	okay	
	angry		

Unit 2　What Are These?

Structures	Vocabulary		Phonics
• What are these? They're monkeys.	monkeys	zebras	Long Vowel i-e
• What are those? They're lions.	pandas	elephants	
• What's this? It's a duck.	kangaroos	snakes	
• What's that? It's a monkey.	giraffes	a duck	
	lions	a rabbit	

Review 1

Unit 3　Is It a Kite?

Structures	Vocabulary		Phonics
• Is it a bat?　Yes, it is. / No, it isn't. It's a kite.	bat	scooter	Long Vowel o-e
• What is it? It's a snake.	baseball	jump rope	
• This is for you. Thank you.	glove	pencil case	
• Here it is. Thank you.	soccer ball	elephant	
	bike	snake	
	kite		

Unit 4　Are They Birds?

Structures	Vocabulary		Phonics
• Are they birds?　Yes, they are. / No, they aren't. They're ladybugs.	bees	ants	Long Vowel u-e
• Is it a frog?　Yes, it is. / No, it isn't.	birds	snails	
	trees	frogs	
	flowers	giraffes	
• What are they? They're ants.	ladybugs	zebras	

Review 2

86

Unit 5 Look at the Whale

Structures	Vocabulary		Phonics

• Look at the whale.
• It's big/small.
   They're very small.
• Are they crabs?
   Yes, they are. / No, they aren't.
• Is it a turtle? Yes, it is. / No, it isn't.
	whale
	shrimp
	starfish
	shark
	jellyfish
	crab
		turtle
		seahorse
		big
		small
		cute
		fun
			Review: Long Vowels
			a-e, i-e, o-e, u-e

Unit 6 Do You Have Red Paint?

Structures	Vocabulary		Phonics
• Do you have scissors? Yes, I do. / No. I don't. • I have red paint. • I don't have crayons. • I have paper. But I don't have scissors. • Here you are. Thank you.	paint tape paper a marker a paintbrush	a glue stick a ruler an eraser crayons scissors	Review: Short/Long Vowels a, i, o, u a-e, i-e, o-e, u-e

Review 3

Unit 7 What Do You Like?

Structures	Vocabulary		Phonics
• What do you like? I like potatoes. • Do you like carrots? Yes, I do. / No, I don't. • I like apples. • I don't like peaches. • I like grapes. But I don't like bananas.	grapes oranges pears bananas carrots	onions mushrooms peaches potatoes tomatoes	Consonant Digraphs ch, sh, wh

Unit 8 Can You Swim?

Structures	Vocabulary		Phonics
• Can you run fast? Yes, I can. / No, I can't. • I can swim. • I can't dive. • I can't ski. But I can skate.	dive swim ski skate jump	run fast jump rope sing well dance well	Consonant Digraph th

Review 4

Midterm TEST 2B

Institute _____

Name _____

Score _____ /100

[1-2] Listen and choose.
잘 듣고 알맞은 그림을 고르세요.

1

ⓐ

ⓑ

ⓒ

ⓓ

2

ⓐ

ⓑ

ⓒ

ⓓ

[6-7] Listen and choose.
잘 듣고 그림에 알맞은 대화를 고르세요.

6

ⓐ   ⓑ   ⓒ   ⓓ

7

ⓐ   ⓑ   ⓒ   ⓓ

8 Listen and choose.
잘 듣고 알맞은 그림을 고르세요.

 ⓐ

 ⓑ

 ⓒ

 ⓓ

[9-10] Listen and choose.
잘 듣고 알맞은 응답을 고르세요.

9 ⓐ Yes, I am.　　ⓑ No, I'm not.
　　ⓒ Yes, it is.　　ⓓ Yes, they are.

10 ⓐ I'm sad.　　ⓑ It's a duck.
　　ⓒ They're lions.　　ⓓ It's a bike.

3 Listen and choose.
잘 듣고 그림에 알맞은 것을 고르세요.

 ⓐ　　ⓑ　　ⓒ　　ⓓ

[4-5] Listen and mark O or X.
잘 듣고 그림과 일치하면 O표, 일치하지 않으면 X표를 하세요.

4 ( )

5 ( )

Final TEST 2B

Institute

Name

Score   /100

[1-2] Listen and choose.
잘 듣고 알맞은 그림을 고르세요.

1
ⓐ
ⓑ
ⓒ
ⓓ

2
ⓐ
ⓑ

ⓒ
ⓓ

[6-7] Listen and choose.
잘 듣고 그림에 알맞은 대화를 고르세요.

6
ⓐ
ⓑ
ⓒ
ⓓ

7

ⓐ
ⓑ
ⓒ
ⓓ

8 Listen and choose.
잘 듣고 알맞은 그림을 고르세요.

ⓐ

ⓑ

ⓒ

ⓓ

[9-10] Listen and choose.
잘 듣고 알맞은 응답을 고르세요.

9
ⓐ Yes, I am.　ⓑ Yes, I do.
ⓒ Yes, I can.　ⓓ Yes, it is.

10
ⓐ It's small.　ⓑ I can sing well.
ⓒ I like onions.　ⓓ I have a ruler.

3 Listen and choose.
잘 듣고 알맞은 그림을 고르세요.

ⓐ

ⓑ

ⓒ

ⓓ

[4-5] Listen and mark O or X.
잘 듣고 그림과 일치하면 ○ 표, 일치하지 않으면 X 표를 하세요.

4

(　)

5

(　)

Let's Go · 2B

Unit 3 p. 23

Unit 5 p. 43

Unit 6 p. 51

2 B

2nd Edition

LET'S GO

to the English World

Word Book
& Workbook

CHUNJAE EDUCATION, INC.

Word Book

UNIT 1 Are You Scared?

happy
행복한

I'm happy.
나는 행복해.

sad
슬픈

I'm sad.
나는 슬퍼.

hungry
배고픈

I'm hungry.
나는 배고파.

thirsty
목마른

I'm not thirsty.
나는 목마르지 않아.

angry
화난

I'm not angry.
나는 화나지 않아.

sleepy
졸린

I'm not sleepy.
나는 졸리지 않아.

tired
피곤한, 지친

Are you tired?
너 피곤하니? / 너 지쳤니?

scared
무서운, 겁먹은

Are you scared?
너 무섭니? / 너 겁나니?

B Read, write, and say.

☐Read ☐Write ☐Say

1 happy
행복한

2 sad
슬픈

3 hungry
배고픈

4 thirsty
목마른

5 angry
화난

6 sleepy
졸린

7 tired
피곤한, 지친

8 scared
무서운, 겁먹은

Learn More

too 또한, 역시	I'm hungry, too. 나도 배고파.
okay 괜찮은	Are you okay? 너 괜찮니?
	I'm sorry. 미안해. — That's okay. 괜찮아.

What Are These?

A Listen and repeat.

monkeys 원숭이들
(a monkey 원숭이 한 마리)

They're monkeys.
그것들은 원숭이야.

pandas 판다들
(a panda 판다 한 마리)

They're pandas.
그것들은 판다야.

kangaroos 캥거루들
(a kangaroo 캥거루 한 마리)

They're kangaroos.
그것들은 캥거루야.

giraffes 기린들
(a giraffe 기린 한 마리)

They're giraffes.
그것들은 기린이야.

lions 사자들
(a lion 사자 한 마리)

They're lions.
그것들은 사자야.

zebras 얼룩말들
(a zebra 얼룩말 한 마리)

They're zebras.
그것들은 얼룩말이야.

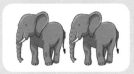

elephants 코끼리들
(an elephant 코끼리 한 마리)

They're elephants.
그것들은 코끼리야.

snakes 뱀들
(a snake 뱀 한 마리)

They're snakes.
그것들은 뱀이야.

these 이것들

What are these?
이것들은 무엇이니?

those 저것들

What are those?
저것들은 무엇이니?

B Read, write, and say.

1 monkeys
원숭이들

2 pandas
판다들

3 kangaroos
캥거루들

4 giraffes
기린들

5 lions
사자들

6 zebras
얼룩말들

7 elephants
코끼리들

8 snakes
뱀들

9 these
이것들

10 those
저것들

Learn More

this 이것	**What's this?** 이것은 무엇이니?
that 저것	**What's that?** 저것은 무엇이니?
they 그것들, 그들	**They're baby lions.** 그것들은 아기 사자야.
friends 친구들	**They're my friends.** 그들은 나의 친구야.

UNIT 3 Is It a Kite?

Ⓐ Listen and repeat. 27 28

bat
야구방망이

It's a bat.
그것은 야구방망이야.

baseball
야구공

It's a baseball.
그것은 야구공이야.

glove
야구 글러브

It's a glove.
그것은 야구 글러브야.

soccer ball
축구공

Is it a soccer ball?
그것은 축구공이니?

bike
자전거

Is it a bike?
그것은 자전거니?

kite
연

Is it a kite?
그것은 연이니?

scooter
스쿠터

Is it a scooter?
그것은 스쿠터니?

jump rope
줄넘기

Is it a jump rope?
그것은 줄넘기니?

B Read, write, and say.

1 **bat**
야구방망이

2 **baseball**
야구공

3 **glove**
야구 글러브

4 **soccer ball**
축구공

5 **bike**
자전거

6 **kite**
연

7 **scooter**
스쿠터

8 **jump rope**
줄넘기

Learn More

What is it? 그것은 무엇이니?

This is for you. 이것은 너를 위한 거야.

a bat 야구방망이, 박쥐   **a pencil case** 필통

A Listen and repeat. 40 41

bees 벌들
(a bee 벌 한 마리)

They're bees.
그것들은 벌이야.

birds 새들
(a bird 새 한 마리)

They're birds.
그것들은 새야.

trees 나무들
(a tree 나무 한 그루)

They're trees.
그것들은 나무야.

flowers 꽃들
(a flower 꽃 한 송이)

Are they flowers?
그것들은 꽃이니?

ladybugs 무당벌레들
(a ladybug 무당벌레 한 마리)

Are they ladybugs?
그것들은 무당벌레니?

ants 개미들
(an ant 개미 한 마리)

Are they ants?
그것들은 개미니?

snails 달팽이들
(a snail 달팽이 한 마리)

Are they snails?
그것들은 달팽이니?

frogs 개구리들
(a frog 개구리 한 마리)

Are they frogs?
그것들은 개구리니?

B Read, write, and say.

☐ Read ☐ Write ☐ Say

1 **bees**
  벌들

2 **birds**
  새들

3 **trees**
  나무들

4 **flowers**
  꽃들

5 **ladybugs**
  무당벌레들

6 **ants**
  개미들

7 **snails**
  달팽이들

8 **frogs**
  개구리들

Learn More

they 그것들, 그들 | **What are** they**?** 그것들은 무엇이니?

A Listen and repeat. 53 54

whale
고래

Look at the whale.
고래 좀 봐.

shrimp
새우

Look at the shrimp.
새우 좀 봐.

starfish
불가사리

Look at the starfish.
불가사리 좀 봐.

shark
상어

Look at the shark.
상어 좀 봐.

jellyfish
해파리

Look at the jellyfish.
해파리 좀 봐.

crab
게

Is it a crab?
그것은 게니?

turtle
바다거북

Is it a turtle?
그것은 바다거북이니?

seahorse
해마

Is it a seahorse?
그것은 해마니?

big
(크기가) 큰

It's big.
그것은 커.

small
(크기가) 작은

It's small.
그것은 작아.

1 **whale**
고래

2 **shrimp**
새우

3 **starfish**
불가사리

4 **shark**
상어

5 **jellyfish**
해파리

6 **crab**
게

7 **turtle**
바다거북

8 **seahorse**
해마

9 **big**
(크기가) 큰

10 **small**
(크기가) 작은

Learn More

cute 귀여운	It's cute. 그것은 귀여워.
fun 재미있는	It's fun. 그것은 재미있어.
very 매우	They're very small. 그것들은 매우 작아.

UNIT 6 Do You Have Red Paint?

A Listen and repeat.

paint
물감

I have paint.
나는 물감을 가지고 있어.

crayons
크레용 (여러 개)

I have crayons.
나는 크레용을 가지고 있어.

a marker
매직펜

I have a marker.
나는 매직펜을 가지고 있어.

a paintbrush
그림 붓

I don't have a paintbrush.
나는 그림 붓이 없어.

tape
테이프

I don't have tape.
나는 테이프가 없어.

paper
종이

I don't have paper.
나는 종이가 없어.

a glue stick
고체 풀 (딱풀)

Do you have a glue stick?
너는 고체 풀을 가지고 있니?

scissors
가위

Do you have scissors?
너는 가위를 가지고 있니?

have
가지고 있다

I have **scissors.**
나는 가위를 가지고 있어.

12

B Read, write, and say.

1 **paint**
물감

2 **crayons**
크레용 (여러 개)

3 **a marker**
매직펜

4 **a paintbrush**
그림 붓

5 **tape**
테이프

6 **paper**
종이

7 **a glue stick**
고체 풀 (딱풀)

8 **scissors**
가위

9 **have**
가지고 있다

Learn More

a ruler 자   an eraser 지우개   a pencil 연필

Here you are. 여기 있어.

Thank you. = Thanks. 고마워.

but 그러나 | I have paper. But I don't have scissors.
나는 종이를 가지고 있어. 하지만 나는 가위는 없어.

UNIT 7 What Do You Like?

A Listen and repeat.

grapes 포도 (여러 개)
(a grape 포도 한 알)

I like grapes.
나는 포도를 좋아해.

oranges 오렌지 (여러 개)
(an orange 오렌지 한 개)

I like oranges.
나는 오렌지를 좋아해.

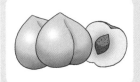

peaches 복숭아 (여러 개)
(a peach 복숭아)

I don't like peaches.
나는 복숭아를 좋아하지 않아.

carrots 당근 (여러 개)
(a carrot 당근 한 개)

I don't like carrots.
나는 당근을 좋아하지 않아.

potatoes 감자 (여러 개)
(a potato 감자 한 개)

I don't like potatoes.
나는 감자를 좋아하지 않아.

onions 양파 (여러 개)
(an onion 양파 한 개)

Do you like onions?
너는 양파를 좋아하니?

tomatoes 토마토 (여러 개)
(a tomato 토마토 한 개)

Do you like tomatoes?
너는 토마토를 좋아하니?

mushrooms 버섯 (여러 개)
(a mushroom 버섯 한 개)

Do you like mushrooms?
너는 버섯을 좋아하니?

B Read, write, and say.

1 **grapes**
포도 (여러 개)

2 **oranges**
오렌지 (여러 개)

3 **peaches**
복숭아 (여러 개)

4 **carrots**
당근 (여러 개)

5 **potatoes**
감자 (여러 개)

6 **onions**
양파 (여러 개)

7 **tomatoes**
토마토 (여러 개)

8 **mushrooms**
버섯 (여러 개)

Learn More

what 무엇	What **do you like?** 너는 무엇을 좋아하니?
like 좋아하다	I like **apples.** 나는 사과를 좋아해.
don't like 좋아하지 않다	I don't like **grapes.** 나는 포도를 좋아하지 않아.

UNIT 8 Can You Swim?

A Listen and repeat. 92 93

dive
다이빙하다

I can dive.
나는 다이빙할 수 있어.

swim
수영하다, 헤엄치다

I can swim.
나는 수영할 수 있어.

ski
스키 타다

I can ski.
나는 스키 탈 수 있어.

skate
스케이트 타다

I can't skate.
나는 스케이트를 못 타.

run fast
빨리 달리다

I can't run fast.
나는 빨리 달리지 못해.

jump rope
줄넘기하다

I can't jump rope.
나는 줄넘기를 못해.

sing well
노래를 잘 부르다

Can you sing well?
너는 노래를 잘 부를 수 있니?

dance well
춤을 잘 추다

Can you dance well?
너는 춤을 잘 출 수 있니?

B Read, write, and say.

☐ Read ☐ Write ☐ Say

1 dive
다이빙하다

2 swim
수영하다

3 ski
스키 타다

4 skate
스케이트 타다

5 run fast
빨리 달리다

6 jump rope
줄넘기하다

7 sing well
노래를 잘 부르다

8 dance well
춤을 잘 추다

Learn More

| jump 점프하다 | I can jump. 나는 점프할 수 있어. |
| but 그러나 | I can't dive. But I can swim. 나는 다이빙은 못해. 하지만 나는 수영할 수 있어. |

Workbook

Are You Scared?

Words

A Match and write.

1 hungry	2 sleepy	3 thirsty	4 angry

_____ _____ _____ _____

5 scared	6 sad	7 happy	8 tired

_____ _____ _____ _____

Practice

A Read and mark O or X.

| 1 | I'm happy. | ☐ | 2 | I'm sleepy. | ☐ |
| 3 | I'm tired. | ☐ | 4 | I'm thirsty. | ☐ |

B Look and write.

Yes, I am.

No, I'm not.

1 A: Are you angry?

   B: _____

2 A: Are you sad?

   B: _____

3 A: Are you hungry?

   B: _____

4 A: Are you scared?

   B: _____

Listen & Talk

Ⓐ Read and match.

1

A: Are you angry?

B: Yes, I am.

2

A: Are you tired?

B: No, I'm not. I'm sleepy.

3

A: Are you hungry?

B: No, I'm not. I'm thirsty.

Ⓑ Look and write.

hungry

sad

scared

1 A: Are you _____? 　 B: Yes, I am.

2 A: _____ you angry? 　 B: No, I'm not. I'm _____.

3 A: Are _____ thirsty? 　 B: No, I'm _____.

Write & Talk

A Look and write.

1

A: Are you _____?

B: Yes, _____ _____.

2

A: _____ you _____?

B: _____, I am.

3

A: Are you tired?

B: _____, I'm not. I'm _____.

4

A: _____ _____ sad?

B: Yes, _____ _____.

5

A: I'm sorry, Judy.

B: That's okay.

A: _____ _____ angry?

B: No, I'm not _____.

Story

Ⓐ Look and write.

| Are you okay? | No, I'm not angry. | I'm sorry, Mom. |

1

_____

Are you angry?

_____

2

_____

Yes, I am.

Ⓑ Look and write.

1

A: Are you _____?

B: Yes, _____ _____.

2

A: Are _____ sleepy?

B: _____, I'm not. I'm _____.

3

A: _____ you hungry?

B: No, _____ _____. I'm _____.

24

Writing

Ⓐ Make the sentence.

1

| . | thirsty | I'm |

····▶ _____

나는 목말라.

2

| happy | . | I'm |

····▶ _____

나는 행복해.

3

| scared | ? | Are | you |

····▶ _____

너 무섭니?

4

| you | sleepy | ? | Are |

····▶ _____

너 졸리니?

5

| hungry | Are | ? | you |

····▶ _____

너 배고프니?

What Are These?

Words

A Look and write.

1

_____

2

_____

3

_____

4
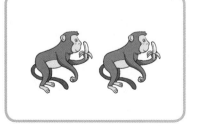
_____

monkeys

pandas

giraffes

kangaroos

lions

zebras

snakes

elephants

5

_____

6
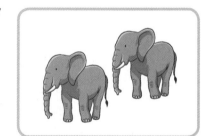
_____

7

_____

8
_____

Practice

A Read and check.

1 They're lions.

☐ ☐

2 They're monkeys.

☐ ☐

3 They're kangaroos.

☐ ☐

4 They're snakes.

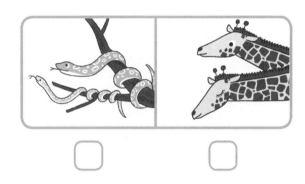

☐ ☐

B Circle and write.

1

A: What are _____?
　　　(these / those)

B: They're _____.
　　　(giraffes / pandas)

2

A: What are _____?
　　　(these / those)

B: They're _____.
　　　(elephants / zebras)

Listen & Talk

Ⓐ Circle and check.

1

A: What are (these / those)?

B: ☐ It's a zebra.
☐ They're zebras.

2

A: What are (these / those)?

B: ☐ It's a snake.
☐ They're snakes.

3

A: What's (this / that)?

B: ☐ It's a giraffe.
☐ They're giraffes.

Ⓑ Look and write.

| these | It's | lion | that | monkeys |

1

A: What's _____?

B: _____ a _____.

2

A: What are _____?

B: They're _____.

Write & Talk

Ⓐ Look and write.

1

A: What's this?

B: It's a _____ .

2

A: What's _____?

B: It's a _____ .

3

A: _____ are these?

B: They're _____ .

4

A: What are _____?

B: They're _____ .

5

A: _____ this?

B: It's a _____ .

A: What _____ those?

B: _____ elephants.

Story

A Look and write.

| They're monkeys. | What are these? | It's a snake. |

1

What's that?

2

B Look and write.

1

A: _____ this?

B: It's a _____.

2

A: What are _____?

B: They're _____.

3

A: What's _____?

B: _____ a panda.

4

A: _____ are those?

B: _____ zebras.

Writing

Ⓐ Make the sentence.

1

| are | ? | What | those |

····▸ _____

저것들은 무엇이니?

2

| are | ? | these | What |

····▸ _____

이것들은 무엇이니?

3

| giraffes | . | They're |

····▸ _____

그것들은 기린이야.

4

| this | ? | What's |

····▸ _____

이것은 무엇이니?

5

| kangaroo | a | It's | . |

····▸ _____

그것은 캥거루야.

Is It a Kite?

Words

Ⓐ Circle and write.

1

(baseball / soccer ball)

_____

2

(bike / scooter)

_____

3

(glove / bat)

_____

4

(kite / jump rope)

_____

5

(scooter / jump rope)

_____

6

(glove / baseball)

_____

7
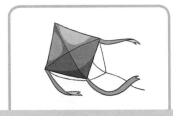
(bike / kite)

_____

8

(bat / soccer ball)

_____

Practice

(A) Look and match.

1
It's •

2
It's •

3
It's •

4
It's •

• a jump rope.

• a bike.

• a scooter.

• a kite.

(B) Circle and write.

1

A: Is it _____?
(a baseball / a soccer ball)

B: Yes, it is.

2

A: Is it _____?
(a bat / a bike)

B: Yes, it is.

3

A: Is it a jump rope?

B: No, it isn't. It's _____.
(a bike / a glove)

Listen & Talk

A Look and check.

1

A: ☐ Is it a bat? ☐ Is it a scooter?

B: Yes, it is.

2

A: ☐ Is it a bike? ☐ Is it a kite?

B: Yes, it is.

3

A: Is it a baseball?

B: ☐ Yes, it is. ☐ No, it isn't. It's a jump rope.

B Look and write.

| No, it isn't. Yes, it is. a glove a baseball |

1

A: Is it a soccer ball?

B: _____

2

A: Is it a bat?

B: _____ It's _____.

3

A: Is it a scooter?

B: _____ It's _____.

Write & Talk

(A) Look and write.

1

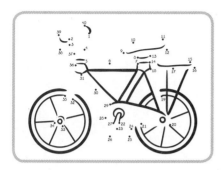

A: Is it a _____?

B: Yes, _____ _____.

2

A: _____ it a jump rope?

B: No, _____ _____. It's a _____.

3

A: _____ _____ a giraffe?

B: _____, it isn't. It's an _____.

4

A: This is for you.

B: Is it a _____?

A: Yes, _____ _____.

B: Thank you, Tina.

5

A: Is it an orange?

B: No, _____ _____.

A: What is it?

B: It's an _____.

Story

A Read and number.

1 **A:** Is it a jump rope?   **B:** Yes, it is.

2 **A:** Is it a bike?   **B:** No, it isn't.

3 **A:** Is it a soccer ball?   **B:** No, it isn't.

B Look and write.

1

A: Is it a _____?

B: Yes, it is.

2

A: Is it a bat?

B: No, _____ _____. It's a _____.

3

A: _____ _____ a glove?

B: _____, it isn't. It's a _____.

Writing

Ⓐ Make the sentence.

1

| ? | Is | kite | it | a |

···▶ _____

그것은 연이니?

2

| it | glove | ? | a | Is |

···▶ _____

그것은 야구 글러브니?

3

| bike | ? | a | Is | it |

···▶ _____

그것은 자전거니?

4

| it | Is | ? | jump rope | a |

···▶ _____

그것은 줄넘기니?

5

| it | is | What | ? |

···▶ _____

그것은 무엇이니?

Are They Birds?

Words

Ⓐ Look and write.

1

_____

2

_____

3

_____

4

_____

flowers

ladybugs

snails

birds

trees

frogs

bees

ants

5

_____

6

_____

7

_____

8

_____

Practice

A Look and number.

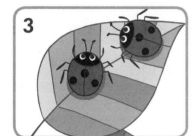

☐ They're bees.

☐ They're birds.

☐ They're ladybugs.

☐ They're snails.

B Look and write.

frogs	ants	flowers

1

A: Are they _____?

B: Yes, they are.

2

A: Are they _____?

B: Yes, they are.

3

A: Are they bees?

B: No, they aren't. They're _____.

Listen & Talk

A Look and check.

1

A: Are they frogs?

B: ☐ Yes, they are.

☐ No, they aren't. They're birds.

2

A: Are they snails?

B: ☐ Yes, they are.

☐ No, they aren't. They're ladybugs.

3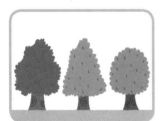

A: Are they flowers?

B: ☐ Yes, they are.

☐ No, they aren't. They're trees.

B Look and write.

ants

bees

ladybugs

1 A: Are they _____?

B: Yes, _____ are.

2 A: _____ they snails?

B: No, they aren't. They're _____.

3 A: Are _____ frogs?

B: _____, they aren't. They're _____.

Write & Talk

A Look and write.

1

A: Are they flowers?

B: Yes, _____ _____.

2

A: Is it a _____?

B: Yes, it is.

3

A: _____ _____ ants?

B: _____, they aren't. They're _____.

4

A: _____ _____ a tree?

B: Yes, it is.

A: Are they bees?

B: _____, they _____.

5

A: Are they _____?

B: No, they aren't.

A: _____ are they?

B: They're _____.

Story

A Look and write.

Are they bees?	They're ladybugs.	Are they ants?

1

Yes, they are.

2

No, they aren't.

_____

B Look and write.

1

A: _____ it a _____?

B: Yes, it is.

2

A: Are they snails?

B: _____, _____ _____.

3

A: _____ they _____?

B: Yes, they are.

4

A: _____ they trees?

B: No, _____ aren't.

They're _____.

Writing

Ⓐ Make the sentence.

1

| ants | They're | . |

....▸ _____

그것들은 개미야.

2

| bees | ? | they | Are |

....▸ _____

그것들은 벌이니?

3

| flowers | ? | Are | they |

....▸ _____

그것들은 꽃이니?

4

| Is | ? | a snail | it |

....▸ _____

그것은 달팽이니?

5

| ? | ladybugs | Are | they |

....▸ _____

그것들은 무당벌레니?

Look at the Whale

Words

A Check and write.

1
☐ whale
☐ starfish

_____

2
☐ seahorse
☐ crab

_____

3
☐ turtle
☐ jellyfish

_____

4
☐ shark
☐ shrimp

_____

5
☐ starfish
☐ shark

_____

6
☐ jellyfish
☐ seahorse

_____

7
☐ crab
☐ shrimp

_____

8
☐ turtle
☐ whale

_____

Practice

A Read and choose.

1 Look at the shrimp.

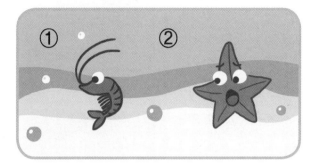

2 Look at the shark.

3 Look at the crab.

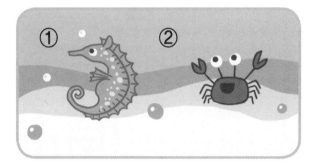

4 Look at the jellyfish.

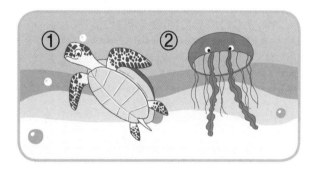

B Look and circle.

1

Look at the (whale / shrimp).

It's (small / big).

2

Look at the (crab / turtle).

It's (small / big).

Listen & Talk

A Read and match.

1

A: Look at the jellyfish.

B: It's big.

2

A: Look at the turtle.

B: It's small.

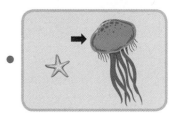

3

A: Look at the crabs.

B: They're big.

B Look and write.

starfish   shark   seahorses   big   small

1

A: Look at the _____.

B: It's _____.

2

A: Look at the _____.

B: They're _____.

3

A: Look at the _____.

B: It's _____.

Write & Talk

A Look and write.

1

A: Look at the _____.

B: It's very _____.

2

A: Look at the _____.

B: _____ small.

3

A: _____ _____ the frogs.

B: _____ small and cute.

4

A: Is it a _____?

B: Yes, it is.

A: Oh, it's _____.

5

A: Look! Are they _____?

B: Yes, _____ _____.

A: They're big.

Story

A Read and number.

1

A: Look at the seahorse.

B: It's small and cute.

2

A: Look at the jellyfish.

B: It's big.

3

A: Look at the fish.

B: They're small.

B Look and write.

1 A: Look at the _____.

   B: Wow, it's very _____.

2 A: Look at the _____.

   B: They're _____.

3 A: Look at the _____.

   B: It's _____.

Writing

A Make the sentence.

1

| the | Look | at | . | starfish |

••▶ _____

불가사리 좀 봐.

2

| turtles | at | Look | . | the |

••▶ _____

거북들 좀 봐.

3

| a | it | ? | Is | seahorse |

••▶ _____

그것은 해마니?

4

| big | very | . | It's |

••▶ _____

그것은 정말 크구나.

5

| small | . | They're |

••▶ _____

그것들은 작구나.

Do You Have Red Paint?

Words

A Check and trace.

1

☐ paint
☐ scissors

2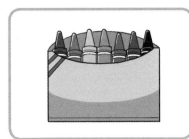

☐ crayons
☐ tape

3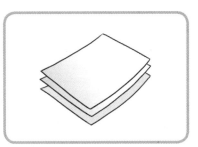

☐ a marker
☐ paper

4

☐ a glue stick
☐ a paintbrush

5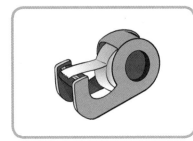

☐ tape
☐ paint

6

☐ paper
☐ a paintbrush

7

☐ scissors
☐ a marker

8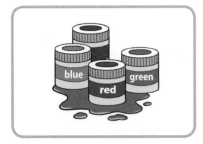

☐ paint
☐ crayons

Practice

A Look and circle.

1

I have [a ruler / an eraser].

2

I don't have [tape / paint].

3

I don't have [scissors / paper].

4

I have [a marker / a glue stick].

B Look and write.

| a marker | crayons | Yes, I do. | No, I don't. |

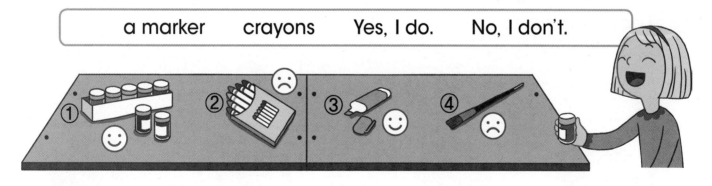

1 A: Do you have paint?   B: _____

2 A: Do you have _____?   B: No, I don't.

3 A: Do you have _____?   B: Yes, I do.

4 A: Do you have a paintbrush?   B: _____

Listen & Talk

Ⓐ Look and check.

1

☐ I have scissors.

☐ I don't have scissors.

2

A: Do you have a glue stick?

B: ☐ Yes, I do.   ☐ No, I don't.

3

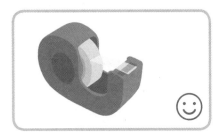

A: Do you have tape?

B: ☐ Yes, I do.   ☐ No, I don't.

Ⓑ Look and write.

1

A: Do you have a _____?

B: Yes, _____ _____.

2

A: Do you have _____?

B: No, _____ _____.

Write & Talk

A Look and write.

1

red

A: _____ _____ have a red marker?

B: _____, I do.

2

I have _____.

But I _____ have _____.

3

green

A: Do you have green _____?

B: _____, _____ _____.

4

A: Do _____ have a _____?

B: No, I _____.

But I _____ a pen.

5

A: I _____ _____ a paintbrush.

Do you have a _____?

B: _____, I do. Here you are.

A: Thank you.

Story

A Look and match.

1

A: I don't have tape.
  Do you have tape?
B: No, I don't.

2

A: Do you have a black crayon?
B: Yes, I do.

3

A: Do you have blue paint?
B: Yes, I do.

B Look and write.

I have ...
1   2

I don't have ...
3   4

1 A: Do you have a _____?

   B: _____, I _____.

2 A: Do you have _____?

   B: _____, I _____.

3 A: Do you have _____?

   B: _____, I _____.

4 A: Do you have a _____?

   B: _____, I _____.

Writing

A Make the sentence.

1

| a ruler | I | . | have |

…▶ _____

나는 자를 가지고 있어.

2

| have | don't | . | I | scissors |

…▶ _____

나는 가위를 가지고 있지 않아.

3

| you | Do | have | ? | a marker |

…▶ _____

너는 매직펜을 가지고 있니?

4

| have | you | ? | Do | tape |

…▶ _____

너는 테이프를 가지고 있니?

5

| you | ? | a glue stick | Do | have |

…▶ _____

너는 고체 풀을 가지고 있니?

What Do You Like?

Words

A Look and write.

1

onions
tomatoes
_____

2

mushrooms
grapes
_____

3

oranges
carrots
_____

4
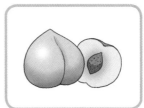
potatoes
peaches
_____

5

tomatoes
carrots
_____

6

onions
mushrooms
_____

7

potatoes
pineapples
_____

8

peaches
grapes
_____

Practice

A Look and mark O or X.

1

I like potatoes. ☐

2

I don't like onions. ☐

3

I don't like carrots. ☐

4

I like peaches. ☐

B Match and write.

What do you like?

1

2

3

mushrooms ➡ I like _____.

grapes ➡ I like _____.

tomatoes ➡ I like _____.

Listen & Talk

(A) Look and check.

1

- ☐ I like potatoes.
- ☐ I don't like carrots.

2

A: What do you like?

B: ☐ I like grapes.　☐ I like mushrooms.

3

A: Do you like onions?

B: ☐ Yes, I do.　☐ No, I don't.

(B) Look and write.

grapes
onions
peaches
mushrooms

1 A: Do you like _____?

　　B: _____, I _____.

2 A: Do you like mushrooms?

　　B: No, _____ _____.

3 A: Do you like _____?

　　B: _____, I _____.

4 A: _____ do you like?

　　B: I like _____.

Write & Talk

Ⓐ Look and write.

1

A: Do you like _____?

B: _____, I do.

2

A: I _____ onions. How about you?

B: I _____ _____ onions.

3

A: I like oranges.

_____ do you _____?

B: I like _____.

4

A: Do you _____ carrots?

B: No, I _____.

A: _____ do you like?

B: I like _____.

5

A: _____ do you like?

B: I like _____. _____ you like apples?

A: Yes, _____ _____.

Story

Ⓐ Look and write.

| Do you like potatoes? | Yes, I do. | What do you like? |

1

I like tomatoes.

2

Ⓑ Look and write.

1 A: Do you like _____?

B: _____, I _____.

2 A: Do you like tomatoes?

B: _____, I _____.

3 A: Do you like _____?

B: No, I don't.

A: _____ do you like?

B: I like mushrooms.

Writing

Ⓐ Make the sentence.

1

| like | I | . | potatoes |

...▶ _____

나는 감자를 좋아해.

2

| don't | I | carrots | . | like |

...▶ _____

나는 당근을 좋아하지 않아.

3

| you | ? | Do | tomatoes | like |

...▶ _____

너는 토마토를 좋아하니?

4

| like | ? | onions | you | Do |

...▶ _____

너는 양파를 좋아하니?

5

| you | like | do | What | ? |

...▶ _____

너는 무엇을 좋아하니?

Can You Swim?

Words

A Check and trace.

1

☐ jump rope
☐ run fast

2

☐ skate
☐ dive

3

☐ dance well
☐ sing well

4

☐ ski
☐ swim

5

☐ dive
☐ skate

6

☐ run fast
☐ jump rope

7

☐ swim
☐ ski

8

☐ sing well
☐ dance well

Practice

A Match and circle.

1

2

3

I (can / can't) sing well.

I (can / can't) run fast.

I (can / can't) skate.

B Write and check.

swim   ski   dance well

1

A: Can you _____?

B: ☐ Yes, I can.   ☐ No, I can't.

2

A: Can you _____?

B: ☐ Yes, I can.   ☐ No, I can't.

3

A: Can you _____?

B: ☐ Yes, I can.   ☐ No, I can't.

Listen & Talk

Ⓐ Read, match, and draw.

1

A: Can you dive?
B: No, I can't dive.

2

A: Can you sing well?
B: Yes, I can sing well.

3

A: Can you swim?
B: Yes, I can swim.

Ⓑ Look and write.

| skate | jump rope | run fast |

	1	2	3
Eden	☹	☺	☺
Kate	☺	☹	☹

		Eden	Kate
1	Can you _____?	No, I can't.	_____
2	Can you _____?	Yes, I can.	_____
3	Can you _____?	_____	No, I can't.

64

Write & Talk

Ⓐ Look and write.

1

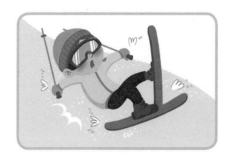

A: Can you _____?

B: No, I _____.

2

A: I can't skate. Can you _____?

B: _____, I can.

3

A: _____ _____ dive?

B: _____, I can't. But I can _____.

4

A: _____ you run fast?

B: No, I _____. How about you?

A: I can run fast.

5

A: I can dance well.

Can you _____?

B: No, _____ _____.

But I can sing well.

Story

A Look and circle.

1

A: Can you dive?

B: (Yes, I can. / No, I can't.)

2

A: I (can / can't) skate. Can you skate?

B: (Yes, I can. / No, I can't.)

3

A: I (can / can't) jump. Can you jump?

B: (Yes, I can jump. / No, I can't jump.)

B Look and write.

1

A: Can you _____?

B: _____

2

A: Can you _____?

B: _____

3

A: Can you _____?

B: _____

Writing

A Make the sentence.

1

`.` `can` `I` `sing well`

····▶ _____

나는 노래를 잘 부를 수 있어.

2

`jump rope` `.` `can't` `I`

····▶ _____

나는 줄넘기를 못해.

3

`can` `I` `.` `dance well`

····▶ _____

나는 춤을 잘 출 수 있어.

4

`you` `?` `Can` `ski`

····▶ _____

너는 스키 탈 수 있니?

5

`swim` `Can` `?` `you`

····▶ _____

너는 수영할 수 있니?

2B